The Riot Grrrl Thing

The Riot Grrrl Thing

Sara Larsen

Roof Books
New York

ISBN: ISBN 978-1-931824-80-4
Library of Congress Control Number: 2019930949

Cover art: Colter Jacobsen

Thank you to the editors of the following publications who published pieces or early drafts of pieces from this book: *Eleven Eleven*, *Dreamboat*, *Where Eagles Dare*, *Mirage #4/Period(ical)*, and *Splinter*. I would like to acknowledge and thank all of the organizers of the New Narrative Conference, Communal Presence, at University of California, Berkeley, where I gave the talk "Blood and Guts and Riot Grrrl or Suck My Left One!" in October, 2017.

Thanks to David Brazil for publishing parts of this work as a chapbook, "After Sappho." And extra thanks for his relentless encouragement in listening to and reading this work many times over. Thanks to Brandon Brown for reading parts of this book during the writing process and offering feedback.

NEW YORK STATE OF OPPORTUNITY. Council on the Arts This book is made possible, in part, by the New York State Council on the Arts with the support of Governor Andrew Cuomo and the New York State Legislature.

Roof Books
are published by
Segue Foundation
300 Bowery, New York, NY 10012
seguefoundation.com

Roof Books
are distributed by
Small Press Distribution
1341 Seventh Street
Berkeley, CA. 94710-1403
800-869-7553 or spdbooks.org

Dedicated to Rachel and Julie

rebel girl you are the queen of my world

"Any appearance
of the
individual heart

is a political
occurrence"

-Kathy
Acker

all text in italics = Bikini Kill lyrics

★

i was a libertine in

the ante-room of Love , some
remember

black (earth?)

UnManageAble crux of femme

I DARED MYSELF TO MARK SOMETHING ON PAPYRI
hunk of flesh salt meat words
rush like a Maenad over
grave-isles garbage-vales thick-crocus mountains &
gut-sad seas
for Space is not easily discerned by Mortals.

hey Sapph, take up yr lyre
play something we DON'T know the words to

Gongyla, Atthis, Andromeda, Amalthea
Anaktoria &

the big violet bruise.

sing abalone-crowned Cytherea eclipse-of-state
whose voice hustles

us scarred shocked abject subversive UnderSung

we fight this society of death

★

even among   radical hoi polloi   i’m not pre-approved
for   credit
only greek has a word   that
means both DEATH & TAXES   :   TELOS

rich guys at riots bore   they take their cash away I & Anaktoria
don’t do   what they say   cashless,

we watch cops,

we train as street medics,-Andromeda notes snipers on
Tribune Tower, takes
City Hall

Andromeda has a secret text from me:

No Honey   No Bee

the Wisdom-Eaters - Deipnosophistae - provide a mansplanation.

I say:

Anaktoria   I say, Andromeda

★

there

a near-trembling ugly

way to be in total loss

of cognition,

numbness to body

I'm songlike engaged in gaps, where the book is of shadow's vermillion. I was not paid, but I understand what I can sweep into my garbage bag. what my sphere will pull together— my mind, my surroundings, my overheards, my books. the way the scene will coalesce in kairotic synergy. the larceny with which I approach my double.

Could life be better? I don't know

anything about re-cognition.
Without a palette, I have flesh to love, I have body of AIDS,
I have to love my body of AIDS, it is to care for, to love.

I have body that endured violence, I wear the body of the women's shelter. I do not want to die. I will not die. With a hand, I am carnal space feeling for real my gliding, stormy body, with the other hand, I write this to you.

how art thou, is yr

jaw clenched up?

★

My pantheon smashes American haunt-my-soul-ed-ness, baptizing projections. The admin binder hasn't been updated. His ghost in my dream says release me. & I release him & I am released. Our practice of rents dare class to elegantly announce: my muscle & organ dance of poverty, decay, sex & death. It's prior to rebirth. Word spread through zines. It's a class issue to be whatever satiated is,

silence=death.

My breeches need to hear that you feel this problem in your body too. That you still hold my letter from 1984. *double dare ya.* I wanted to use materials that stunk. Things you never hated. It's a carrier pigeon culture. I have an IV but you never saw it. I'm interested in the gaps. In not punking out. If you want to see, you must DIY – do it yrself. DIY & IV is the riot of a vibration that collaborates with Joan Jett to make the best fucking 7 inch you ever heard.

★

I AM A GOAT

i'm moving in two directions

a sauna in flux
grasping at body
fleeing up in the air
a rope w/ no causal tie
an agent un loosened
in limb & skin

what do i do o matrix
to keep on living in this junkyard?

i am a goat.
i have become a goat.

Anaktoria.

★

While I was waiting to have the abortion I was reading Andrea Dworkin & it felt like hell; how about you? I'm not. I hold on to my Size Queen tape because they were a local band who put out their own tape & if I lose the tape I will lose them forever. It's fucking near impossible to write this. I've been dead except I woke up & needed money to buy clothes.

News of ghosts butter

the party's alcohol that's why all your

bullshit is the phenomena of honey.

I think I wanna take you home & live alone. I just became that way, a double absolute at the Fake Haus sitting on the floor next to Kathleen with her sports dude knee-highs. *it's about being in love*. The corset over a Jam t-shirt. If you want to look at my asshole yr gonna have to look all the way in, if you want to see my cunt, yr gonna have to see all of it. Turns out you see what you want to see, not my fat ass for real. The ginger blossom convexed into a half space that contoured what was out of my turn. I was never the type to stay so corpse-y. *it's all the same thing. it's all the same thing*. I slid out of Rimbaud's vaginal cock. & I wore this red blue & white t-shirt mini dress with low top doc martins. Not the boot kind. My taboos had an empire built around them. My taboos had AIDS & laid their tender precious bodies on the white lawn, whited out; how yr zine didn't print right, how you couldn't read the words. Like that.
Whited the fuck out.

★

WhoIsAnaktoria?SapphoRemindedOfAnaktoriaInSappho16Anak toriaWhoIsNotHereWe RemindedOfAnaktoriaWhoIsNotHere AnaktoriaWhoIsNotHereGirlFriendOrAbalonePerhapsLoverO SapphosWhoCanTell?EmbeddedInSappho16EmblemOfLove APoemRecallsEndlessWarOfHomericPeriodSapphoImmortally StatesYokeMateAsIfOutOfVeryMouthOfAphrodite"IWentLooking ForYouOuOuuu"ItsOnlyLoveLeadUsSojournOutOfFauxEqu alibriumOfAccustomedHorror"SoDismal"OnlyLoveTurnsCruelty HabitAroundVerse=Around=ATurningLyreTheStringed Instrument SapphoPlaysThisIsLiterallyRevolutionaryLyricSong

AnaktoriaWhoIsNotHereIs"GoneGoneDownByTheOcean"Where IsAnaktoriaAnaktoriaWhoIsNotHere"StartedToCry"AnaktoriaWho IsNotHereTheFeminineAnaxWomanWhoRulesRulesWhatWhom OnlyKnowWeThatSheIs"GoneGone"In"AnotherDimension"No ThoughtOfWorldLeftBehind"WellYouKnowWhatIMean"Anaktoria WhoIsNotHere"IsWashedUp" SapphCallsHerNameAtthisGongy laAndromedaLookingFor"GoneGone"InMytilene

MaskOfNameLittleHoneyPreservedNeverReturn"GoneGone"High VoltageSweetBitterLoadedFoamKelpShell"AnotherDimension" "IWentLooking""GirlIsWashedUp".

★

—falling-in second floor of the Fake Haus in West Philadelphia. It was farther into West Philadelphia than I had previously ventured. A group of us walked the thin old streets with trash strewn around & huge magnolia trees looking for the venue which couldn't have been more than a large punk house that used their upstairs for shows. I saw Bikini Kill play twice, this was the first. The second time was on top of the Drexel parking lot with Size Queen but that's another story. At the Fake Haus, I can't remember who opened. Lots of people where there, but it wasn't stuffed – you could easily sit on the floor in the middle or back if you wanted. The energy incredibly huge. I was still in high school & my parents definitely didn't know I was seeing a show at a dilapidated house in West Philly. When Bikini Kill came on, suddenly everyone rushed to the front, especially the girls & as we danced & sang the floor moved up & down in waves like an earthquake was happening. An earthquake was happening. Seeing Kathleen & Tobi & Kathi & Billy (who stayed low key) broke something in me, something old & inherited. Kathleen & Tobi both screamed into the mics.

Kathleen dropped her voice low, *does it scare you, we don't need you,* then higher, *does it scare you boy,* then shrieking & cracking, *THAT WE DON'T NEED YOU?!!* Julie & I lost ourselves jumping & dancing. We held hands & then the crashing movement of the whole crowd broke our grip. It was awesome to see Bikini Kill change who played what instrument, like, every other song. There was no true leader of the band. Everyone collaborated. Plus it was messy. It was art. It was libidinal. There was a point. I remember that Kathleen wore a pink & black corset over a t-shirt over a thrifted looking tennis skirt with white socks pulled up to her knees & chucks. I only mention it because

how she looked blew me away…at some point she took the t-shirt off & it was just the corset. I had only seen women in corsets on TV, & then they were always dressed as
an object for men. Kathleen owned this look & it was punk as fuck. It was so empowering. I could own myself. I could own my sexuality. & I could also go raw, rage, have my own band or zine or whatever. Sweat became my aura. I could feel every song in my bones. What happens when a 16 or 17 girl encounters something like this? Of course, I had the cassettes, the zines, I devoured them. But when the performative is present & it's all happening in around you like a force that razes structures, when the floor is going to fall in, when *we don't need you to tell us we're good, don't need you to say we suck*, & patriarchy, capitalism, violence, being an object,…starts to collapse…inside me…starts to collapse structures—

★

look out into vastness of sea at Mytilene resonant with overlook
to Alcatraz

Prison cool eternity of the Pacific, sailors who died, all the
Sapphos who stole

fucked worshipped unruly & unmammaled you can't keep lyin',
Mytilene,

volcanic blood femme have no sex no gender they are IRIS fire
who truly

STRUCK the water ?

★

On the other hand, I had to confront what I was writing & I had to confront the sweat of your t-shirted body & your hair matted to your face. My blood & surrealism is not bombastic at core. Layers of reality are nervous, thick. *I can sell my body if I wanna - god knows you already sold your mind.* My guts locked into an art of readiness. Even when I sat there with that burgundy bottle dripping down my fingernails. Stuff comes out when you're not looking. *Is that supposed to be doing that?* I can't let it come out. My desire & distrust marries people I hardly know so much so I film the 16 mm of where this all started. (*silence inside of me*). With burgundy hair, & an unbuttoned thrifted top. My breasts finally joyful, plump, bold, a bunch of marigolds aiming their revolution, who taste. The law was never clear on the class argument of appropriation, Shakespeare, Virgil. Honeysuckle ejaculate that drips not shoots. *It feels fucking blind.* The sister was conventionally heterosexually pretty, a kind of Suzanne from the Bangles. Traditional narrative & the rise of the bourgeoisie, French fucking words I can't fucking spell. We rubbed bodies oceanically in memory's revision. My inner dialogue was afraid to be overpowered & on the other hand it said rhetorically, mmm, hmmm, yeah. In memoriam to identity, my book report stated that if I don't experience it, it must not exist. I never wanted to be the Great American Writer. I became a secret man, dived into a place of patriarchal pre-eminence. But it tasted toxic, contaminated tap water. I thought, what is a man even? I felt sad for them, I hung up the phone. I became a so- called me, the one with the miscarriages & misfires & blood & burgundy shafts. I looked her right in the face, I saw Kathy, I saw me.

★

no honey no bee

"i shall be released"
no honey no bee

i shall be released
no honey no bee

i shall be released
no honey no bee

i shall be released
no honey no bee

i shall be released
no honey no bee

i shall be released
no honey no bee

i shall be released

no honey no bee
i shall be released

★

Oh … Mama …. i cannot get up for work at 7

Aphrodite I am dead-broke upon a HONEYed

lover

★

I like being ill-behaved in the trembling deadlock of a horror show. She dials me back in the slasher movie where everyone moves their bodies in slo-mo & a chanteuse draws out her secret body. Is someone following me? The dark gorge behind my eye is working class, visionary & semi-sweet. We were talking a fragile myopia. Witches are kept alive there, & there are funerals every day. It leads me to this. She picks up her amp, looks at me & walks down the concrete driveway. The Autobiography of a Secret Amber. It's honey, sweet & I have salt in my mouth. Is she hung as a gift? "Do you really think you're ready, Buffy?" I asked her name & she turned it inside out. & then it was discontinued. *Suck my left one*. You held small bottles of whiskey that made yr fingers look long & crooked. Part of the nightmare is what can you do after you fucked in my blood. Here is my Lecture on the Divided Self. The gravest moment is the hottest, there is no way to shut up or back down or not dance. If I get back into the dress, it was before this time. I cut up vintage pieces on problematic ego, another timeless curvature of scoring. My dream was divisionless, the man would not intellectually back down.

A light, fearful sound. It's the music that happens to your mind, being hungry, I wanted to die & so I said you should die. A good little post-modernist punk rock scum.

★

(EROS limb-loosener splays me out
sweetbitter   anarch ic   creature   swarms in)

o beautiful graceful one   you seem to know what   who   eros is

O Aphrodite.

this article is about the Greek goddess of chaos.
for the Greek god of love, see Eros.

for the goddess of love, forget dudes & turn to page 114.

★

O fuck it's national poetry month oh wait fuck. Let's submerge that why fuck suddenly the Lord of Death eats my potluck. I have these flash drives stuck in like tampons, saving all uterine blood. Don't write properly, sing properly, not *all the rage on Nothing Incorporated*. I punch at the lacunae. The holes in identity & personality. I redress the posture of tumults with a self-addressed stamp to tenderness & I a woman talk a whole lot more. This business of printing things on your own is a revolutionary act. So we did—repeater. In the practice of fictioning, I was threatened with metamorphosis. & Jean approached from behind & witnessed the bullet wounds. He let them spill onto toilet paper, cardboard, regular paper & books. His kiss transferred me into the future of bones. My feelings wear Jean's shirts & further agitate my trial of grief. We blindly foretell & it is nasty & it is true & it is here.

★

step outside the one-dimensionality of the tribe   it was
slaves   who were
first to Write   in Greece   the rulers   just talked.

shadow casting

no animal   fat   on my plate

hecatomb: “dream-fluff donuts”

★

how punk fucking rock the door swings open, unocculted of anguish, the light secret dance. In the depths of this nakedness a nude Betty rejoices just above the water at sky. Mermaids are Marys, the myrrh, guarding the bitter unfathomable spiral. They say she is unreadable, her books unreadable. In every detail sublime, nude, what the witches might say & what you never ever hear. What the witches might say. Every gesture, yellow leather roses. In the end, death was short, oxblood. I rush out of the party & descend the stairs. Space is an indication of my relationship with you. Kissing booth. Climbing the chain-link gate. I am a mermaid crawling in the wake of hours. The invisible feeling that flashes you existent. What is that supposed to mean? "You came back Wrong." Shut-up. Blessed be the Sluts, like, many-ass times. She is the composer of the scenes, & other stories of Ego Death. I did that once, lost my grip on purpose & dived into this supersexual body of earthdirt. IT WAS FABULOUS. "From beneath you." I am born in early Autumn in the great eastern sea bored. I am moved to Red Rocks then I am moved to the Western Lands where I was reinitiated into the Living. When color lands, it is yellow.

Don't you know, I don't belong to you. Yet somehow I seem to persist.

True as a weekly income.

★

you & i we   are in the middle void

among this not mortal tableware   i would eat the little
mother
transcribe rain & milk

i said my heart feels like a nerf ball, it is the dry color of
pinot noir, it's taste:

milk & honey & salt.

the letters above me are from mother Eos,

sweetworded

send me a taste of ruach   a bead trans parent in glass

you & i   are in the mortal void

a paradise of glass   it means the one who shakes
the figs
from her Lydian tree   did you love the bridegroom
more than me?

★

Dear Sapph,

Yoke-mate, I went looking for you I lost my phone near the ocean. You have probably texted me so many times. Washed up. I went looking for you, down near the ocean, I went looking for you.

Some say Eris & I was listening to Patti Smith thinking of you.

Some say these cargo boats, some say the port of Oakland when we went there on foot, some say Redondo Beach is light-who-makes-my-body-drop- sublime, most beautiful on black earth. Black earth in my palm. They told me that girl is washed up. I went looking for you ou ou. Most beautiful on black earth.

I say Anaktoria.

I say it is whatsoever a person loves. Any of you. It is what you love.

I say poems I say abalone. Started to cry went in my room. I went looking for you, just standing you were gone gone everyone was singing girl is washed up from Mytilene, are you gonegone

I say it's what you love. Everyone gets this, its easy. Even Helen she was gonegone her husband her child went looking for you off to Troy never return into my arms. Led her away with such light. Everyone was so sad. Cavalry.

Smiling angel. I reminded now started to cry of Anaktoria who is gone. I'd rather see her return into my arms with her lovely walk the spark of light on her quick face, another dimension you know what I mean. I'd rather see her than any Lydian chariots or dudes with A-circle flags. It'll never happen. I went looking for you. Impossible. But I pray…to the unexpected

★

dare it all, double dare it   listen to the silence or to the radio
because even

without a dollar bill in my pocket

    i dance   in a void   i am   & almost dead

green pungent grass grips   seizure   sweat   in trans
mission

they say it can   be un concealed   stuck in this mythos

dance with stillborn tongue   carry the dead for a month until
labor induces

Orpheus heart-bone   tongue breaks like a wave   wildfire
ingrown under skin   "love will tear"
                                        tear open the dead through living space

OMG—
        i can't talk!   when you laugh   my heart flies out!

you speak   honey-tongue   "I've lost control again"!

★

I ground bones to make my bread. Debt that slays. In the sixth moon, every one of my friends say the same. Tracks 1, 2, 4 & 5 recorded by Ian MacKaye at Inner Ear summer 1991. I entered high school that year not giving a damn for any cent or dollar. Does rest in peace have no sanctity to you people? Rich parents, green Saab with the top down. Her mother said, maybe Sara doesn't want your hand-me-down eye shadows. That's what matters. I came in the window by habit, rainbow-feathered with spit on my sleeves. They were rolled up in the manner of Genet. Truth is, I was delighted to be drag at 13, clutched close the hand-me-down eye shades, shades that lurk the New York Dolls. Let your bones drop. I need to get the fuck out of the suburbs. The ephemeral wilderness of indispensable ruptures, strangers, my inhibitions resourced from the censor. They were stealing? Your body must be the nasty companion that carries liberation's spring. She draws her story into mastery's history. It's a reliquary. Note to self: Oh dear, go back to yr zines, write yrself *outta me*. Lay yrself into some inscriptions, cipher it out, lick a stamp (flag upside-down), launch it out in the American mail.

★

Little sister's Book of the Dead:

AnaktoriaDoesWhatABodyCan'tDoAuroraBorealisOurWalkTook
MeSouthwardRomanCandleToArcOfProteanLightBeMyBabyMy
LittleBABYBabyCornerOfFlora&Isabella

EverythingTakesSoLongLongToWakeUpToHouseToSpeakToFill
BucketsBottleRockets& CoalLongToSetFireToAllOldWays
LONG TO TUMBLE BEES FROM HIVE SO THEY KILL WITH
THEIR STRONG

★

the mind is a cloak

Sophia Rose,

        perhaps rosette-ish   i am simply acknowledging this

i don't want to suffer & be aware   grace comes near to me
marries me to paradise

like a lily in the precinct of dew eros unGOVERNABLE
comes piling
  in

WAYS TO CROSS OVER   via aphroditic mounds:
sun-bath, walk, rub cup of dirt

  i go to sophia rose

for a pre script ion   to memory   if i taught memoria: maria
misercordia

★

all these things come from extremely far away, they have good clientele but the cloak trails out,

a huntress cosmology.

compassion imagines the toughness, the depths, fleeing from the axe or axiom of carnal space. she is no longer on view. she says, that's just Love, the father the bird, the mother the earth principle. & i tumbled down into it. am i getting enough exercise?

"Spike's completely in love with you." It's a good time for quarry-able materials, for Iris who plants the je taime. stella polaris, sophia rose.

rainwater comes like fire effacing my first steps. it's volcanic ash, obsidian. any color of it is volcanic ash & then tumbled & then put into my hand. I plunge my roots down into earth & spew shit there. Wash out with rainwater. Bring up Light,

give it to you,

"in the form of a sister"

★

CallHerWaveOfBITTERWaveNotAfraidOfDimensionMariaMind
Don'tConnectToHolyMaryLineageDon'tWorryWhereItBelongsLin
eageWiseDon'tStephanieTheDawnDon'tStephanieTheMoonDo
n'tStephanieTheSelfNotAboutRegeneratingSelfWeaveFloatIn
StephanieSpaceVeryIntentionalProtectiveWorkToCreateSpecifi
cIllusionHolisticStephanieImageHangUpThePhoneForGreater
GoodBetweenWorldsWritingInZoneToOvercomeSelfMythology
MythologyOfOthersStephanieTheAntiMortarMeditateALotSteph
anieMeditateThen WriteInPiecesFigureItOutLaterGiveTruthTo
MemoryNotFacts

StephanieAllowsGreatAcceptanceOfDeathBeAgileIncorporate
BeingTheyAskIsThisIcyFeelingAboutEternityWhatSeaFoamSalt
CallFromAlaskaCaretakingIsEasyNowLaAbeja

★

you & i talked about it all Kythereia
in reverie:

you are not on the earth as you suppose

★

—who disappeared back into what crimson resurrections happen at the show where Julie & I met him. I hesitantly became apostolic in a dulcet watery gutter. There was in my future a fluid score of redwood, madrone, oak & berries; not here. Here it is sweat, tater tots, & other people's mothballed thrifted jackets. & for you, who may be killed, coming out of the darkness into the sublime razor-thighed carnival. Against what or whom? All night diners in the parlance of South Jersey. We sprint around each other's bodies acting as-if. I was born in a hecatomb. So I ask you once again, am I inside or am I outside? *it's all the same thing.* But there are other factors. Solitude's magma swallowing its curse in chili fries & light-speckled pavement. I saved the ticket in a shoebox which is lost. I offer this dim paragraph as dedication to Mon who I remember. Fervently I marry an imaginary band full of women named Kim. The uncarved pansexual body is a runt body but for this. The Troc was in Chinatown two blocks past the Gallery mall. In line for the show we traded zines. *we've got to show them we're worse than queer.* It's a question of impossible acrobatics, not supply & demand. It's the scene of the earth writing a passé secret. "My defining feeling about him was that he had never been a child but had come outta the womb a teenager. What was his zine called superstar forever."What happens next is we swipe death black scrawl & pin-to boards of genderfuck, elevating fuckedness to beauty-space. We are teenagers & thus cannot get in upstairs. I'll just let it burn. Someone yells, girls move forward, girls forward, girls to the light-flickering front—

★

for I am an enemy of the forms of this world

which no longer bind me as Punk

mole is my future ancestor

I EAT YOUR HATE LIKE LOVE I EAT YOUR HATE

LIKE LOVE

I EAT YOUR FUCKING HATE UP LIKE LOVE

★

StandInReedsFormILikeItThatWayWhoCanHoldWhatYrPaintingW
aysBodyRiseAsIFeelAboutYouIComeThruAHimalayas&DownThr
uGreeceAnklesSoreAboutYouAboutYouIFormlessThisForFormT
hisFormlessnessPetalsTheRockInGoodMeasureToLoveAnotherPe
talMinglesInBlueMilk

★

—such elegant surroundings were not the forte of the pilgrims of the PATCO train. I order a fried chicken sandwich with mayonnaise & wilted lettuce at the corner of 8th & Market. *I don't owe you all nothing. Who was me,* I guess I'll not know, a rogue bone structure, a *feminist-dyke-whore-I'm so pretty-alien* from before I was born. PARLEZ VOUS code fucker zine. That Burger King where the pigeon almost chokes on a fry. What makes me weep. Keith Haring. That masculine fucking chicken sandwich that crys & sighs on the other side of the underground journey of Camden to Philly. Vicious art of the army navy store just blocks away. *Your side of things. yeah.* I wear the olive green t-shirt to bourgeois school. Vicious silence of suburbs. Vicious chirping of the birds tamed, matte, mounted by the neighbors. I live by the train tracks (no, really). Everyday all day the PATCO train to Philly marks its light across my walls, the way out, go towards the light, what my father (of Philly) & mother (of Camden) worked to get out of, I want in but in a different way. I am letterstruck. My mother xeroxes all my zines for me. *What are you afraid of.* My schoolmates drive Saabs, wear The Limited. GIRL VIRUS. Fugazi in Chinatown & Ian MacKaye threatens to stop the show if dudes up front stomp, elbow, mosh. I mean something here; not just some girl. I have in my arms zines to give out. Send yrs here, point. I'm taking the Rough with the Smooch. The other place is the Philadelphia Record Exchange. I drop zines from my arms there. Come back to New Jersey on the PATCO with seven inches marked $3.95. I read innards on the train. The train speeds past the hospital where I was born. Our LADY OF LOURDES. Bernadette who prophesied at Lourdes, her Vision was rogue, of healing. She refused to shut the fuck up, birthright. *How does it feel, it feels blind—*

★

MagicHourSheSaysMyHairIsMezclaSunNectarABlisteryUnlook
ableColorOLadyLetThemStayLetThemStayYeahYeahYeahYeah
PleaseDoOneThingOrIsItLazuriteIAmMyselfLapisLazuli&AtHeart
OneCouldEnterTheHeartWaterRagesVioletBlue
TheMindThisSimpleStormingDiamond ThatFeelsTheSame-
AboutYo uAboutYou

IComeToC'estLaMort

ItIsAllWaterYouMayHoldWaterYouMayNotHoldWater

★

—on the floor of my bedroom, which was covered in xeroxes from zines glued to the wall. I played my punk or indie cassette tapes on the stereo on the floor. Had my tapes all neatly aligned & organized in a little white bin next to the stereo. All my favorites were in front: Bikini Kill, Heavens to Betsy, Team Dresch, Velocity Girl, Tsunami & a number of mix tapes from my friends. Mix tapes always told a story through songs & the order of the songs recorded on them. Not that we thought about this that much as the receivers-we didn't. As the givers, yes we thought about it, it was practically the whole point of even making a mix tape for someone. The story was usually one of two things: the mix tape tells the story of how the giver feels about the receiver, whether friendship or love; or, the mix tape tells the story to the receiver of who the giver is, what they are like & what they are into. It reflects them. At some point, I got a mix tape with a yellow piece of paper fitted into the plastic cassette box that would make a little squeaky sound when you opened it, from a girl named Maija who I never met but who I traded zines with in the mail. Some of my favorite songs of that time period were introduced to me by Maija, like "Suki" by Unrest, "Bury The Hammer" by Beat Happening & "Gigantic" by the Pixies. The mix was titled on the side of the cassette PUNK'S DEAD & I KILLED IT! To Sara love from Maija, with stars to dot the dots in her name. I'm holding it in my hand right now. I keep it in drawer in the closet which I rarely open. When I do open the drawer I love to see that there are songs on these tapes that never made it to Spotify or YouTube, songs that live & die on those cassettes. Wednesday, Size Queen, A Roger 7. A semi-secret history I know of only because I was there. They radiate some residue of a time & place I can now see only in my mind, & most of all a girl who engaged in this time

& place, who was someone alive, passing through the world.
It reminds me of the Juliana Hatfield 3 tape I loved:
Become What You—

★

what does it take to raise

flame trouble

she who is dead

a snake of my   real mouth

a fawn beLoved one

she comes with a garnet stone

                    wrapped continuously

upon her neck

what measure comes
        Moon Bull

is one's earth fire

        another fire for the KingEarth

I would like to show   my sculpted tail

★

Mercy for myself, I was raw & it felt right in my body. My body of salt & dust, the one I was on my way to writing, *she's so very I-don't-care*. My eyelid was a deliberate mistake, & *I want it now.* I ate blood nevertheless, fire of love, maxim of the dog, stench of sex & blood, without a reckoning. I left where I came from. Human time both sped up & slowed down to a whisper, fluttering my body with ointments, hurricanes an image akin to telepathy, rays tremendums, bones unclassified. Every road brought me back to the uncharted place where I started. I could never really apologize for anything because my self was already rubbed away in brine. I wore my faded black-grey Chucks to the gym where the girls played guitars. Drums, amps, all of it set out on the gym floor, no stage. Carrie Brownstein whirled her guitar. We are level in art of noise & dance. Do you know what it is to eat blood? Congealed in the refrigerator as a luminary. I continuously sprint back to a practice that I don't yet know, against what prevents me from seeing.

I scribble it all down like a monster from another land. I was in a café where people talked & did their homework - laptops & cell phones were not a thing. Somewhere in my body, a perfect ghost of Virgo, looks out.

★

My body is all of history, all of gossip, all of culture. She is a territory of war. Then you must go forth, fall asleep in the ointments. Lobsters & crabs & alien crustaceans attack my body & I hear myself call out: help me! What descends on me will be innumerable, will count out the divisions of the stars according to their names. I just want to rock this guitar. I read your zine for the images cut out of where history hollows out. The Earth not only your Mother, she is your Lover. I have charged this with my mirror in all the years since. The moon blazes with translation.

★

Which area in your life could use a new point of view? The next morning we ate hamburgers & spit on each other's corpses. All eyes were on her of the mod dress with the pudgy tummy. "Happy birthday, Buffy." I tried to pull off the masks but that's never been my forte. Lights of the party went dark & I pirouetted fingertips.

(codeswitching from the murder of winged limitations).

The moon invites us to become besties through inner, outer & secret slums. it makes our bodies sisterless, nothingness & I blank out on a tongue. I softly kiss her smug face. If we could just face our own incongruity. By now you probably want the salacious story. You don't own me, (Joan Jett cover). I serve right tumult with my defamed beyond-body, besides-my-body, become-body. If I have text messages, let them be my mantra. That's how lost I am in contemporary neighborhood, how fucked I am, how fucked. Did you plan that consciously?? At 10 am, we drank beers on Red Rocks, hotly drunk. I enter the party house through the party portal in my hairless mind. Do you know, *what it's like to be alive?* Work from the inside. I slid up the narrow stairs & stood near the window. Apprentice to protean feelings. I wore a tube top - I don't know why. Aesthetically, we are wily. My revisionist memento mori actuates a scene where I am tougher, hotter than the haunted non-feminist shame feelings battering down the harbor. But we were Punks & that's what mattered! And thus carry a variety of nets, roll down the slope, are scavengers, sorcerers, makeshifts (like me!).

★

enchanted ocean

i have been

awake

an hour loam

spring is Aphroditic i'm trying to be more Empress-centric,

dear Mali,

& less counting of the $6 in my checking account

you know, more

Sea Punk

i believe in the radical possibilities of pleasure babe

where the chains drip off my tits

ocean engulfs all

spangled objects & i fly to Andromeda

★

I was made to Levitate

in oblivion

passing currents Hunan Restaurant shot traffic rain-ocean

16th street

authoritarian spatial smoke-song a shadow a corpse

I confused the barman with a $10 roll

(probation twilight) of quarters I refract thru

glass twilight

PUSH THE NEEDLE

confer with one's supposed-self oysters: no cash, no

sure socket to debit card Limbo even — I definitely know
I am dead a gem
extracted from earth
cool unlike the Hot Mess I am

Queen of Swords suffers most of all Queens.

★

The dark lace of autumnal shudders on the herbs & Rimbaud looks far off past the top of my head crown of stars & flowers. I've entered the lily now & there is no return, born more ancient now, makes me weep like a dog. I've taken up residence with the Punx. Alive on paper, her brow, her face, her damaged bangs pushed off to the side with hunger for greens. Don't you forget it.
What the fuck is written all over your pretty face. Come on. I'm fucking dreaming again the inner skin of my beloved, the doorway to seclusion, rebelling me into adulthood. What did you mean I was a paranoid Queen wilted & tight with fear. Let's go back to our meeting point; where the iris's splay out with a trust fund of whores. I make the bleeding bigger with untamed body ready for scribe. I tried to pull off the masks of Moses— *God, we're having fun!* Turns out this time the chorus was full of men. Again. I watched us from the back of your hand this eleventh moon, near twelfth moon, Scorps, snap a photo of the table of Tecates. & then your throat wretched in my bathroom & lost yr balance in headstand & I saw our dead friend with indigo eyes. I acknowledge that now. *Maybe i liked you*, why don't I show you how I quiver how I lose control. I want a staggering face. I believe in the radical geraniums, feathers. She punched out the mirror, blood smeared down into the moldy sink. I still had a plane to catch. *I don't fit into yr dumb words.* Just become one with The Everything & forget it, OK?

★

your eye

pretty as kale

on the soppy sea

where

my treasure lay

out

tentacles et. al.

★

Like a camera the darkness of our fair sex fills us with light. We don't understand how it decided who is saint, beneath strange moons. It is true honey is no longer honey, notepads invented by death, standing on the street in cut off shorts & Doc Martin mary janes. *So we're going to play a new song for you & we don't know how it goes but it might work.* Punk rock is the second condition of saying adieu. A mystic fireball burns mouth. Let nothing go unsaid. We want redistribution, we want a black bass guitar, we want to ruin the bassline in our band, FUN, forever & ever in the present. *You don't make all the rules.* We overlook the skin, the spoils attuned to bone. Team Dresch rock it so hard in the dance studio space. Rolling back into being metamorphosized...is this how erotic love feels? Lost in developmental chimera. Darkened, wet, emerald grass, this bardo. Our demi-face a cord to no surface, no face, a password *outta me*. We hold benedictine palms, conjure static grey images of Kaia in the high school photo room of the art wing. We are a mess, always ragged in hair, markered up with black scrawl on our arms.

★

this garland strangles out the part

of dude who wrote of Sappho: " She is reputed to have been short,dark and ugly."

feel the fuckery of men who steal in on unmanageable words

feel this: fuck you, I fly to Anaktoria

★

It was a brief stay with the flesh always knowing what you want. The meat sullies up your board if you spill the innards while cutting. I did that a lot, put my childhood to cook on the stove & witness the struggling, bequeath the witness, in moments of limbo vanishing all of it like a volcano. Here I spare a thought for the dark underside of my psyche. *& I am not some lame sorority queen taking you home to meet my Daddy.* I really look forward being a hot fucking mess today. A proof that I paradoxically open before me, a cyclone, *the you I show to you is just a lie.* I forgot all the books I usually plunder. They love me but it is in no way gentle. The cycle of endless shelter & movie-time daggers. Bikini Kill played on top of the Drexel U parking structure under an open sky. Size Queen opened, four queer punks who I heard were all lawyers. I still love their cassette tape, ungettable now, just a local Philly band. I desire to live in a tangy, undistributed light of worldly edges & elevated rabble. To fillet a fish properly you curl the knife up around the ribs, it is not necessary chop off the head. *did you tell them everything I said?* I convulsed & screamed under the zodiac of animals on top of the parking garage. I am a witch & a monster & an alien. I am a fish sliced under a silvery Mercutio. Do I speak of yr descendants because I am them in punkitude, so much so that lyrics are undecipherable? "Punk must be a thing you have to get into in high school to like." I wore the corduroy brown front-button skirt I stole-borrowed from Julie & the cap sleeve pajama top from Thrift Town in Pennsauken. My chunky black platforms met the concrete with panache, expressed within themselves how to vibrate more fully than foot & body with the vicissitudes of city seasons. Punk lyrics are cryptography whose substance is the debris that strikes euthanasia where it festers. No wonder you don't understand a fucking word!

★

irises in Camden

every body   had   them

"IF YOU ARE SILENT ABOUT YOUR PAIN THEY'LL KILL YOU & SAY YOU ENJOYED IT"   says Zora Neale Hurston

Amy was al most   my   name   Beloved   the one who must be loved

I can't write it straight, not straight. We rub your oiled feet with our hair, brush it back, become a whore in composite. Who is beloved to whom? Questions of monstrous proportion, synonymous with uncleanliness. I was the first to deny her malaise was anything Other & I

I am the protagonist   or the supporting   character ?
in the flecked   pitch forks of mothers the   zeitgeist of time

even upon awakening,   I interpreted as punk the trashed
bouffant   we need guts   ecstasy   spiritual union with

★

Our house was yellow until it was blue. There were attic pockets throughout the house, a hobbit door in the kitchen that opened the wall & I stepped in. That's how I found out our house was built without electricity, had gas lamps. Little One was calico, she lived in the pre-history of the house. Our house had black & white linoleum kitchen floors which I fainted upon before catholic school. Our house had a under-the-stairway in where I kissed, in where I listened to Kitaro, in where I read Kahlil Gibran, in where I decorated a secret place. Any fatigue is absolved into interim space. Feelings simple & naïve, under stars near the garden, billions of candles in the high east gather like rainwater. I'm not confiding secrets. Our house had a staircase in where I was supposed to walk down, someday as a bride. Our house had a staircase in where I recited poems. When in fact I was a foreigner to myself. The quiet at night was our house & the sound of the refrigerator. The reflection of my body in the glass sliding doors. I could not fully see a woman who is much older and peers in from the other side of the glass from a place that hasn't happened yet.

Darkness outside where the cat meows.It's incredibly holy, the spool of night. It obfuscates nervous feeling yet does not have a name. Preserved in intimacy, as disruptive a readout on monologue. Perhaps I glued it all together. Perhaps burrowed in alchemy. What was our house but a place I became sometimes-I. Perhaps I have a name but never said the name.

★

Dear Gongyla,

You are here with me, with your laptop you apologized for bringing & I have my laptop & we are writing. You are drinking chai with almond milk, & I am drinking a latte with soy milk & honey & lavender. There is a graceful choreography & a clunky one, to be with pain.

We ended up talking because there is so much to say, & you have dropped me off again at home, I stepped out of your car in my salmon colored rain boots into the flowing gutter & the water parted in waves around my enclosed foot. A body sometimes reminds me of those cabbage wraps with all the meat & rice inside, thin skins in a bed of tomato broth. Steven said something about "a mad dash through heavenly realms," something about being "liberated from being sourpusses".

★

The radiator is another person in the room, a person who is softly dreaming. The blessings of body-mudra gesturing in space, it's a kind of touching & intimacy with others. Am I including the peripheral visions stuffed around the corners of my memory or am I drifting off log-like to another place? When I wear my glasses, rather than my contacts, I cannot see the sides of anything & am sharp-focused, though I appear small-eyed. I have until 10 pm tonight to be writing, that is my direction to myself, that when David comes home soaked from the rainstorm, & he steps dripping atmospheric rain onto the black & white tiles of the bathroom, & he begins to disrobe of his jacket & his backpack & his shoes & his socks that will reveal his chilly pink & cream feet, that will be my little chime alarm, my egg timer.

★

There is sedentary presence & there is mobile presence. Sedentary is the here- now. Mobile is the dance, the pilgrimage—external to a place, or internal around the energy centers of the body. This was all in my notes from class.
Anaktoria, who is not here. I love you. Does love call out the bones? Up from the absence the grave. It cannot be closed, the gap, forgotten, dismissed. Love is action, flow, movement, Lynice says "Back it up with your life."

★

We did a feasibility study & found my subject too limiting. Now I have to deal with people for the ethical treatment of werewolves.

Kathy:
This letter will be received by bones. Like a lobster receives with her claws the flesh, I entered the army/navy store with a sane sense of decorum & left as a glacier. Some say bodies melt piously down but I know the messenger Vinny (née Vinius) will approach you in drag with this nude clutch of poems in the after-world. In the tide pools, what men destroy is hot in my flesh, our mother, the dirt. Adios Hades—the spring's cursive letters swallow me in honorific. This portrait com-muniqué poses a dopey question, one that dudes made up. We sallow whores haven't given up; our healing is in the nature of scripture. What I have written I have writ-ten. I let the bones drop to clitoral hood. Willow is an invisible nerd who witches out. "LOVE OVER FEAR; LOVE OVER MONEY $$$." Do you not beg for unlimited space? You wrote The Black Tarantula after Genet. My song is hidden in variegated muscles.

Then who maintains the poem? A person called

★

—love going to the Trocadero. It was in Chinatown & I would take the PATCO train from Ashland with my friends. My first show ever was there, Fugazi, 1992. Philadelphia's Chinatown was all yellow lights at twilight, narrow streets, old stone. Julie, Rachel, Phil & I bought Arizona teas at the corner store & wait in line in front of the Troc. I handed out my zine to the assortment of kids going to the show: adorable indie rockers with striped t-shirts & shaggy, often faded manic panic colored hair (pinks! blues! pastels!), hardcore kids who mostly wore black or grey & disaffected faces…they further subdivided into multiple groups, straight-edge kids (bold X's sharpie'd on their hands), Hare Krishna vegan hardcore kids…, there were the older punks whose heyday was more in the 80's but there they were, Riot Grrrls of course (this was my jam), & then always some kids who were kind of nerdy or artsy & perhaps this was their first show…just figuring out the scene. At some point early on, all of us were them. I remember Kathleen Hanna saying something like this one time from the microphone. The word "poser" was a thing back then. Kathleen said that no one came out of the womb Punk Rock. I handed out my zine to anyone interested or who wanted to trade. This included my friend Mon who I believe Julie & I met in line at a show. I had a few zines, but my favorite one was called IF I SMILE AT YOU THAT DOESN'T MEAN I DON'T THINK YR A JERK. I photocopied photos of 50's wives cooking dinner or 50's pin-ups looking at the camera & collaged them into pages of teenage rumination & punk album reviews. My family home address in NJ was scrawled—

★

can we just have our own Island of Lesbos? srsly

where Kathy is the nymphomaniac & I am both Toulouse Lautrec & Rosa La Rouge
half-rotted in the dead letter if it's all the same to you I'll make our home

of whale bone
crab claw
& seahorse spit & we'll make signs that say:

refuge for everyone!

yay to phenomena!

yay & yay & yay & YAY!

★

Dear Amy,

They say when your Nan died, that's when you went off the rails. Well, what the fuck do they know! They never knew you, couldn't feel what you felt because they made you an object, hated alive, loved dead. Fuck Society!

I am cold & my back teeth are set hard against my jaw. That Janis line from I Got Dem Old Kozmic Blues Again Baby, "the worst, you could say, oh, about meee ee eee, is that I'm never satisfiiii eedd ooo ooooooo oo oooo oo oo." As I write to you, I hear your North London voice repeating all these words as I type. "It's rather common, isn't it", you said, meaning your speaking voice. You said the elocution lessons "didn't take." Incarnational being is a bitch, isn't it?

Amy means beloved or the one who must be loved. According to my parents, it was almost my name. When you performed Beat It on television with Charlotte Church, you sang it fucked up, forgot words, totally punk. You screamed, raspy. The sound board turned your microphone down. You were rumored to be black-out drunk. Meanwhile, Charlotte conjured her operatic voice perfectly, just the way I hate. You were a fuckin' mess, hair a mess, a fucking trash goddess. You slash the safe propriety of this performance, the sanitized sanity of it.

Slash, you spilt it's blood. Slash, blood on the ballet slippers. It was universally panned, but I saw Riot Grrrl. You put the contra in contralto.

"Singer Amy Winehouse died watching YouTube videos of herself after vodka binge, inquest hears." You were an artist, reviewing your work, & that's how you died. You are the only dead person I have addressed so far. Don't worry, I won't ask what the living can't comprehend.

Amy, Beloved, one of my mothers is gone. She worked her whole life in a garment factory, sewing mass produced clothes. Her husband worked in the factory at Campbell's Soup. You were a singer, younger than her granddaughter. Sometimes I wear your winged eyeliner to the coffeehouse to write.

★

It’s as if my life burst out blushing in error, a phantom on a
minefield, weird, searing, not me. The residues mingle with fate,
twisted spasms of teeth & socially crippled bones, corporeal light
on the brink of the fantastical. I walk in the form of sorrow.
I am a quantitative feather, locked up in an overturned garbage
can, crummy, capital, I put my arms around

★

This is the secret, the sudden rise to life. Which sign, an act of birth, with mine? I wear the drag of wisdom, fucking pissed, fucking depressed. Its' true everything is not ok. Citrine core, a mitochondrion of apparitional identities, lacerate & transfigure. Work from the heart. I wear an anchor pendant around my neck. I hope you submit to mud the way that you submit to bone. Am I writing this. History of the holy cinema. I hope you can go deep underwater, you can be a sailor of bone & mud. American flag is bones in mud under water & you must. There is no pain like show.

★

Atthis, to you

we should trash

all pretense

in a streak of quartz   full of piss

&
sea workers   vignettes

thousands-resplendent
as-long-as-you-want!

★

I snapped out a Tuesday pill, eat it then go, is it Tuesday?

It's the Day of War & Men of Sky. Nerine & Minerva preggers go off together to consort, raise the baby, raise a ballroom of hell. Who is home in the pleasure of wealth. My ancestors worked a thousand bonds in the network of the servile feeling the sense, the soul, the bodily & phenomenological substances unwoven, streaming the light from a source that loves them to death. A simpering wind in the jacked up window, a causal tie to my aching fisticuff shoulder blade. I am writing altho I am done writing. Minerva effaces the mind with her militant focus upon its logos, brand names. I say, I will only shop at thrift stores. Only wear woven shirts worn as vests & men's jeans. Mens is mind. My Grandmom worked sewing clothes in a factory, we picked her up at building number G. Who stitches the symbolic world together. *past the billboards & the magazines*.

★

what will be dared
in lieu of dull silence
powers thru dead loads
radiantly zeros out

we live beyond our means
we work 9-5's
every girl is named Sara
we live beyond what's dared

our means made of silence
Andromeda texts not for me
or honeybee eyes
pure sleep of sweetbitter

sweetbitter seems
so much like   flowering cilantro
or how I break   when she sings
What have you taught me? Nothing.

LOOK AT WHAT YOU TAUGHT ME YOUR WORLD HAS TAUGHT ME NOTHING.

★

Thanks for the spiritual download of the rape protection kit. It's going to be a bloody week for those fuckers. Six months of jail is "a steep price to pay for 20 minutes of action", the rapist's father stated. I unpeel the grape slowly, the skin in one long strip of purple. The parasite with nasty long fingernails eats my skin while I'm still alive. The mushy inner core of the grape, an eyeball. I was dumpstered and. Coming to writing. I refuse to stop my three novels. I was going to stay home. I was not going to read this. I was going to read. Onions, stinking the cutting board. Stay here. And stay with this. White onions, I cry. Sulfuric acid, sulfur. I want control over my H-E-double-L. To find the bull in the rock. *White boy, don't laugh. don't cry.* French lentils, green cumin. Cook at high temp with coconut oil, cook with high heat oil that pops. They'll say, in what way did she deal with rape culture in her book, was it at vanishing point, at disappearance, where it always is. It was screamed the fuck back. Not this time. I can't feel the lower half of my body. Roses hung to dry, arched back, lazy eye, a drum, a sunglass. A convicted rapist in the news. He is white. He is young. He has money. *You really had to be there.* He is an athlete. He is an academic. How else is he a Subject, let's see... what else can we say about his full in-dispensable young white male life...? I check my pulse. Blood. I check my onions.

★

Adrienne said I am hard to get to know. It makes knots, thorns in my desperate manly virtue. No, in my feminine leprosy. It makes knots, thorns in my weight of wretchedness, my tribe's protective love. There was a huge amethyst dildo. Amethyst! A crystal that plunges cold into my very essence composed of dough, I might have gotten by, but the fly was undone. We were naked, fences to each other still. I will make you see that you are not much of a seer. Or rather, that you are, our forms loosely based on the musical, loosely hung from a bone hanger, loosely dangling from light's muscular journal. It is said that I don't need you. I am you, I think. I know that in Adrienne there is a piquant luminosity. Perhaps I am the one who never took off the mask. I was not open. I huddled into Derrick's car with my hemophiliac puppy. Who I loved like a religion. Pot smoke spun into the air behind us. A pillar woven into a decade. What might I do now as a diamond singer? We carry the ones who we came along with.

So why do I remember so many objects, those objects that emote experience, experiences I barely recall. Again, I say I don't remember my life.

★

someone may remember us

as limbslackeners in the

exiles of grace

moonset upon Pleiades
garlanded in beginnings

Now I look around
& wonder where my girlfriends are?
I WANNA BE YOUR GIRLFRIEND! the lovely altar!
in light of the sun!

someone may remember us
as wisdom-mongerers in the
exegesis of heart-stone

what do I remember what do I re member

neither honey nor bee

★

Time—especially—is patriarchal. Everything's canceled because everyone's depressed. Forages for ancient cemeterial howls. I stepped in the white apartment with high ceilings. Everyone moves, disobeys another presentiment. The earth turns on its polaris, no, it revolved up-side-down. It's the summer they're stealing all the iron works that cover the windows & doors in Philly. Sweltering. I touch the plastic cover of The Hot Rock, girls hailing a cab, touch Self-Titled that begins with *double dare ya*

double dare ya
girl fucking friend

★

Am I from SEA or am I from BEE or
Am I of stream or am I of bitch or Am I on BOUGH or
am I from FIRE or Am I
mother of am I earth
Do I crash in RAGE WAVES
Teeth full of grubs
Am I complain of my Wage Am I spoken not
spoken to
Am I anoint Myrrh of oil Do I split Mother
BLUE
or
Avoid Ash & Soot
Am I gilded plague or do I bear
the Dislodged Scepter
Am I comb out the Hair
or turn out his Stomach
Am I mad at the bed of love or do I harness all
things
Has Hades in its Margins & Jails
FAILED TO CAPTURE his prisoner

★

It's time to begin with words, sewn from hemlock, engaged upon air, a woolen air complete with number and letter, hewn of ancient wood, from a time unlike any time, whose voice destroys all voice, amplifies all voice, and calls out to the reader with light-quick qualities and metrics, all the series of the heart. I cry with words of this being on the couch, under the stars but indirectly, with slight tummy ache, who hears Bach's cello suites and the movement of the pen. The curtains are turquoise and there is a seashell on the altar. The body smokes with intelligence, cancels all debts, elides all promises to classification, I am one with my vow, I am one with the catnap on the couch. We both have jetlag and I need to say so many times something like, "do you think that's why were tired, jetlag"? This pillow is from Christmas, though it is mid-June, mid-summer, nearly solstice, everyone I know struggles to not psychologically die, not to pass out. I guess I will always be wandering, a pilgrim with a home who

peonies

dahlias

hydrangeas

feeding your demons
flood
what makes you

★

karma and circumstance in our own hearts, our proper hearts, the body's freshness unveiled as we touch dead ones. What's on view? No one said anything to me about vipers or walking side-ways on the walls.

I came here to call you forward

to fix the blasted printer, to age me

in grace among sirens and earthquakes and cumulus clouds and August eclipse.

People were erudite then holiness prevailed. My eyes are heavy as the Duomo.

Activated and kissed upon by unquantifiable megawatts of glory, the joy of all that is.

I must have been an elephant in one of my former lives and had my heart broken by hunters—it is too tender to talk about. The tender, open space of a pool of water in land where we gather, trunk to trunk. I must have been a woman burned because I hear snaps of twigs and cackling of crowd I pray to Hidden Ones for help. As I go unconscious I see herbs in the palms of my hands, years ago. I am swimming in the sea where heat plows me forward.
Love is an ocean of sea creatures with ugly, odd faces whose ancestry is ancient

who swim in middle earth
I am grateful

The city is a moon of light in distance
All things complete and perfect now
right now
the vegetables in my fridge

sleep tight

I am old, again, my life as a saint

★

the wheel of gnostic light. So here we are again: light. I ate temperately, and hung earrings on the wall. I threw out the old heating pad. I swept the floor. There's no path to coolness in this deadest of situations. The soul of the city is gone they have eradicated it with money.

Narrative is really hard.

Sensorium is really hard
So-called realism is really hard

and rather
unsatisfactory

the mouth on my hand speaks

it says something

hard to hear   something like

★

garland / girlfriend obviously

to you I White Goat

let's unearth ourselves to Ojai get the fuck out of here
I will not let
you
brushy mountain womb

get the fuck in brackets of waterfalls slathering my body

I can't make it in that white place wet with dew

I am ruled by Mercury like you I must speak

★

—lived near the railroad tracks. No, seriously, I really did. I walked up & down Railroad Blvd dreaming that the commuter train held the key to all of my dreams. With scotch tape, I hung my anonymous one-page one-off zines up in the Ashland train station near where you buy the blue & white tickets to Philly. They were girls-with-knives-collages slash declarations-of-rebellion slash punk-quote-ridden slash poetic-prose slash top-10-band lists. It was my own mini self-made ticket the fuck out of there. It projected me into a future of a cooler self, it was a Riot Grrrl 16 year old vision board. It was always anti-climatic to hang the finished sheet. I poured my whole self, my heart, my energy, my anger, my libidinal rage into these things. & when they'd go up, the imaginary audience I'd invented in my head seemed to somehow shrink as I watched random Jersey commuters zombie-like scuttle through daily motions. Or young kids like myself, but ones who weren't into art or the underground music scene, who were maybe going to Philly to shop at the Gallery Mall. I wanted to shoot off into the atmosphere! I wanted to scream like Kathleen! I wanted to blow apart mediocrity with my art! Somehow the Ashland train station in Cherry Hill, NJ wasn't doing—

★

SeaPunkAphroditeCyprianQueenPinkQuartzFoamInA
LitanyOfKelpWhoDanglesEmeralds:

IWillHaveSungACanticleInAFutureLifeIWillHaveLivedBeyondOur
MeansIWillHaveLoosenedMyLydianSandalInABathOfPorcelain
IWillHaveHadNoTokenWithMeIWillHaveBeenCalledADykeBitchIn
TheRecessOfOriginIWillHaveCameInATheaterTooColdToBear
IWillHave DancedWithAQueenWhoNeverHeardOfMytileneIWill
HaveTangledMyNailsInHisHairIWill HaveResistedByWalkingPast
TowersThisEveningIWillHaveBecomeAPoetNoOneCanSeeI Will
HaveRecycledMyBottlesInAnEarthquakeOfMirrorsIWillHave...For
...TheSea

★

cups isn't real   eternity BONES now

(when in doubt, throw it out)

Don'tBringMoneyStripAuthorityEmpire

"Take time during the meal to enjoy the Wisdom Croissants & to talk about everyone's

'rules to live by'"

★

UNMANAGABLE   wakes me   endless
hum

Hermetica of Awful State written in glass at   tops of trees
we hear only a SEA SPARROW

DiamondWind crashes out paycheck debt paycheck- debt-
debt

It's not so hard to understand this, srsly, buck the fuck up—
open the door, our Alcatraz pours itself upon you, little sister

Stories are real,not you,not yr lashed tongue

not the strap

not   every way this is stolen from me nowhere matter where

★

The polity has been shot through with vice, well hell I guess anyone might say that. Recall that we used to gather, with bottle of wine, & radical pamphlets & fugitive chapbooks, I recall laying on the upended hardwood floor one late night & Jason was dirty drunk & Lily was laughing on the couch & I was secretly mad at someone & someone else puked in the bathroom & someone else kicked the wall in & the older women neighbors who have had enough came & screamed at us over Rihanna &

those cheaply made boots because I was unemployed & couldn't afford shoes. I was in the early stages of getting fat. I had "No Scrubs" as my ringtone on my flip phone.

I loved to gather. & there is a gap. Lights strung across the gap.

★

—what does it mean to be Riot Grrrl? Is it to scrawl in black sharpie SLUT or BITCH on your tummy because my friends & me never actually did that. Spent hours pasting zines together or swinging on the elementary school swings across from Rach's house or screamed Huggy Bear lyrics in a parent's borrowed car or pasted cut-from-zines photocopies of Bratmobile onto the bedroom wall. We just wanted to kick down the door with heavy Doc Martin mary janes. Say fuck empire, fuck Sony or whatever big record corporation, fuck clothes from the mall! Fuck rape culture, fuck money! Fuck high school!

Yes to subculture, to DIY crooked messy aesthetic, to thrift stores and seven inches made of red vinyl. Yes to this stereo with homemade Hell Kitty stickers, yes to sneaking off on the train to Philadelphia, yes to queercore, yes to stapled zines all over my pink bedroom rug. Yes to dilapidated punk houses, yes to all night diners. Yes to girls with guitars, girls with glitter, girls with big glasses, girls with short skirts that are for me NOT YOU, yes to baby barrettes, yes to baby t-shirts stretched over me, yes to hair dye, yes to "I talk too much, I laugh too loud, people stare at me when I'm in a crowd". Yes to fly by night indie labels. Yes to fly by night indie or punk bands where all the band members are also in a slew of other favorite bands. Yes to girls to the front, yes to—

★

"I WANNA KNOW WHAT LOVE IS…

I WANT YOU TO SHOW ME"

this song by Julie Ruin came on in the car the other night while we were parked & we sang along to the sampled chorus.

I WANNA KNOW WHAT LOVE IS Nadya from Pussy Riot talks about having love affairs in prison. "You have to fight for your joy." She said you have to fight for your joy because they'll try so hard to take it away from you. Pussy Riot is not so much as band as a movement, she says. Anyone can be part of Pussy Riot.

& I was thinking of Riot Grrrl & the Kathy Acker talk I'm about to give & yet to write

& how punk is an ethos & poetry & how do I fight

for my joy

BLOOD & GUTS & RIOT GRRRL or SUCK MY LEFT ONE!

WRITTEN FOR THE NEW NARRATIVE CONFERENCE, COMMUNAL PRESENCE, UC BERKELEY, OCTOBER 2017 .

I'm going to start this talk by not talking but by playing you a song by the band Bikini Kill. This talk is about Kathy Acker & Riot Grrrl, Riot Grrrl is a genre of punk, & punk music can't really be explained, it has to be experienced. There is also a xerox of the lyrics of the song from the 7" that I'm playing so you can check out the lyrics.

> ASIDE (regarding Bikini Kill's lyric sheet) —You will note David Wojnarowicz's Burning House in the upper left hand corner, connecting this to street art & AIDS activism & you will notice that the words "Her House" have been written in, adding another dimension to the significance of the image.

[play "Suck My Left One"]

Riot Grrrl was a feminist movement in the early 90's punk scene that blew apart the male hetero voice dominance that had existed in punk since its beginnings in the 70's. Riot Grrrl bands' lyrics took on issues of sexual abuse, rape, domestic abuse, sexuality, patriarchy, & female & queer empowerment in their song lyrics, style, zines & political activism. Bikini Kill famously open their self-titled EP by yelling out [play beginning of Double Dare Ya] *We're Bikini Kill & we want revolution grrrl-style NOW!!!* Lots of bands were part of the Riot Grrrl movement —bands like Heavens To Betsy, Huggy Bear, Bratmobile, Team Dresch, The Fakes, to name a handful—but to pare things down to bare bones for this talk, my focus is on Bikini Kill, the lead band & inarguably the most important band of Riot Grrrl.

Like all punk, Riot Grrrl was defined by the punk DIY ethic, which rejected mainstream, capitalist culture & valorized "Do It Yourself" (DIY). That means taking the means of production into one's own hands from record labels to fanzines (zine for short – fanzines are handmade cut & paste, xeroxed, stapled underground magazines. They often include messy images appropriated from mainstream culture & recontextualized to subversion).

Bikini Kill started at Evergreen college, probably in 1991.

Kathleen Hanna, lead singer of Bikini Kill:

[play recording from the documentary "The Punk Singer"]:

> "I discovered Kathy Acker, the American writer & I went to this workshop that she did. & she told me why do you want to write? & I said because nobody has ever listened to me my whole life & I have all of this stuff that I want to say. & she said then why are you doing spoken word, you should be in a band, because nobody goes to spoken word except for people who go to see bands. So I went home & I started a band."

& Kathy Acker:

> "I hated the life which I was living at that time; I hated the society; I didn't differentiate between the two. I thought that if my friends & our society didn't find a way for adequate change, we would die & quickly. Some of us did die. I wanted radical change, however it had to come. At

> the same time I was aware that writing changes nothing on the larger political scale. One reason for this, of course, is that those who are most oppressed are often either illiterate or rarely read. Literature, especially novels, is written by & for the owning or the educated populace. Here is one reason why the novel is one of the most conservative art forms in our century. I wanted change, but I had no adequate tools or weapons."

We take the tools, the weapons into our own hands & remake them, DIY.

I mentioned before that Riot Grrrl or any punk needs to be experienced. It is about what's said, but more than that it's about HOW IT IS SAID, how it is experienced. Riot Grrrl doesn't just interpolate you into what's happening—it is already what is happening to you, as a woman, as a queer person, as a nerd, as a misfit. To prepare for this talk, I was looking around my apartment for a book that came out a few years ago about the history of Riot Grrrl. It's called "Girls To The Front" by Sara Marcus. I couldn't find it anywhere & figured that I gave it away. & then I thought, wait a minute. I don't need the book. I was there! I experienced it. I WAS fucking Riot Grrrl. I don't need someone to feed me the narrative history of what happened. I am Riot Grrrl. That's Riot Grrrl.

Kathy:

> "Marginal," "experimental," & "avant-garde" are often words used to describe texts in this other tradition. Not because writing such as Burroughs's or Genet's is marginal, but because our society, through the voice of its literary society,

> cannot bear immediacy, the truth, especially the political truth.
>
> I've never been sure about the need for literary criticism. If a work is immediate enough, alive enough, the proper response isn't to be academic, to write about it, but to use it, to go on. By using each other, each other's texts, we keep on living, imagining, making, fucking, & we fight this society of death."

Kathy's work also demands to be experienced—what demands it is the form/forms she experimented with throughout her life. Cut-up, appropriation, especially appropriation of the patriarchal canon are subverted into new works. Her works show what's up from the point of view of a rebel girl. Or from prismatic points of view, unstable. Kathy lied a lot, I often hear. So did Genet, so did Burroughs.

One of the things Kathy's work has in common with Riot Grrrl is saying what shouldn't—by troll guy, dude oligarch, mainstream patriarchal capitalist standards—be said. The narrative, if it can be called that, belongs to the collective or as Kathy says in her essay "A Few Notes on Two of My Books",

> "If there is a self, it's probably the world."

Kathy talks about not meeting the demands of the literary establishment. She says,

> "Burroughs never bores, for he & the other writers I think of as in "that tradition," "the other tradition," "the nonacceptable literary tradition," "the tradition of those books which were hated when they were written & subsequently became literary history," "the black tradition," "the tradition

> of political writing as opposed to propaganda" (de Sade would head this list) (here I am not talking about American literary tradition), do what Poe said a writer should do. They present the human heart naked so that our world, for a second, explodes into flames....Any appearance of the individual heart is a political occurrence."

Again, Kathy writes,

> "If a work is immediate enough, alive enough, the proper response isn't to be academic, to write about it, but to use it, to go on. By using each other, each other's texts, we keep on living, imagining, making, fucking, & we fight this society of death."

Bikini Kill screams in Jigsaw Youth:

> *I can sell my body if I wanna! God knows you already sold your mind....you think that I don't know, I'm here to tell you I do. You think that I don't know? I know the truth about you!*

or most explicitly in Resist Psychic Death:

> *I'll resist with every inch & every breath, I'll resist this psychic death.*

I don't repeat, I insist.

[play clip of "Resist Psychic Death"]

We opened with Bikini Kill's song "Suck My Left One":

Mama says:
You got to be polite girl
You got to be polite girl
Show a little respect for your father
Wait until YOUR FATHER GETS HOME.

Punishment of Father with a capital F, patriarchy. In Blood & Guts, Janey's interactions with Father show her interaction with patriarchy. Father calls the shots. Father decides to leave Janey & be with Sally. Father doesn't want to deal with Janey. Janey is dependent on Father financially. Father would like to fuck but would like Janey out of his space. Janey's narration:

> "LASHES MAKE ME NO LONGER MYSELF...
> LASHES, AS IF THE WORLD, BY IT'S VERY NATURE, HATES ME...
> CAUSE OF LASHES: THE SURGE OF SUFFERING IN THE SOUL CORRUPTS THE SOUL..."

When Janey moves away from Father, she joins a gang, The Scorpions.

"The rest of THE SCORPIONS were growing the sameway I was.

> We started out making trouble. Early one morning we rode in a stolen van into a Connecticut town & busted into a hardware store. We threw everything in the store out of the door.
>
> We don't hate, understand, we have to get back. Fight the dullness of shit society. Alienated robotized images. Here's your cooky, ma'am. No to anything but madness."

& she starts to have to work:

> "I hated most that I didn't have any more dreams or visons. It's not that the vision-world, the world of passion & wildness, no longer existed. It always is. But awake I was disconnected from dreams. I was psychotic."

[Play "New Radio"]

> *Turn that song down, turn that static up, come here baby let me kiss you like a boy does!*

Like the messiness of THE SCORPIONS break-out of "the dullness of shit society", Bikini Kill's song New Radio defiantly turns up the static. Not satisfied with the categorical orderliness of phallocentric capitalism, Bikini Kill takes the power position: *come here baby let me kiss you like a boy does.* & they say simultaneously fuck you to authority. Sex & pleasure are smeared on the parent's bed, on the dream-space of Authority itself.

What can save one's life, under domination by patriarchy, by capitalism? *Baby boy, you can't kill what's fucking real.* Flat out rebellion, making space where one can speak. Boundary making around the dream-space. Kathy's Janey maps out her dreams. In "Blood & Guts", we get dialogue, thought-reads, drawings, dream-maps, poems, translation, journals & collage. "If there is a self, it's probably the world."

The self speaks non-linearly, without dualism,

> *I will resist with every inch & every breath*
> *I will resist this psychic death*

There's more than two ways of thinking
There's more than one way of knowing
There's more than two ways of being
There's more than one way of going somewhere

The self speaks without attachment to self but with solidarity to the inner heart space, that which would be crushed by society, with solidarity to others who are also self.

I'm going to read to you from the Riot Grrrl manifesto. There are multiple versions of this as all women involved in Riot Grrrl were encouraged to write their own manifestos. Here is a version most often cited:

> "BECAUSE us girls crave records and books and fanzines that speak to US that WE feel included in and can understand in our own ways.
>
> BECAUSE we wanna make it easier for girls to see/hear each other's work so that we can share strategies & criticize/applaud each other.
>
> BECAUSE we must take over the means of production in order to create our own meanings.
>
> BECAUSE viewing our work as being connected to our girl-friends-politics real lives is essential if we are gonna figure out how we are doing impacts, reflects, perpetuates, or DISRUPTS the status quo.
>
> BECAUSE we recognize fantasies of Instant Macho Gun Revolution as impractical lies meant to keep us simply dreaming instead of becoming our own dreams and THUS

seek to create revolution in our own lives every single day by envisioning and creating alternatives to the bullshit christian capitalist way of doing things.

BECAUSE we want and need be encouraged and to encourage in the face of all our own insecurities, in the face of beergutboyrock that tells us we can't play our instruments, in the face of "authorities" who say our bands/zines/etc are the worst in the US and who attribute any validation or success of our work to girl bandwagon hype

BECAUSE we don't wanna assimilate to someone else's (boy) standards of what is or isn't good music or punk rock or good writing and thus need to create forums where we can recreate, destroy and define our own visions.

BECAUSE we are unwilling to falter under claims that we arereactionary "reverse sexists" & NOT THETRUEPUNK ROCKSOULCRUSADERS THAT WE KNOW we really are.

BECAUSE we know that life is much more than physical survival and are patently aware that the punk rock "you can do anything" idea is crucial to the coming angry grrrl rock revolution which seeks to save the psychic and cultural lives of girls and women everywhere, according to their own terms, and not ours.

BECAUSE we are interested in creating non-hierarchical ways of being and making music, friends, & scenes based on communication + understanding, instead of competition + good/bad categorizations.

BECAUSE doing/reading/seeing/hearing cool things that

validate and challenge us can help us gain the strength and sense of community that we need in order to figure out how bullshit like racism, able-bodieism, ageism, speciesism, classism, thinism, sexism, anti-semitism and heterosexism figures in our own lives.

BECAUSE we see fostering and supporting girl scenes and girl artists of all kinds as integral to this process.

BECAUSE we hate capitalism in all its forms and see our main goal as sharing information & staying alive, instead of making profits or being cool according to traditional standards.

BECAUSE we are angry at a society that tells us Girl = Dumb, Girl = Bad, Girl = Weak.

BECAUSE we are unwilling to let our real and valid anger be diffused and/or turned against us via the internalization of sexism as witnessed in girl/girl jealousies and self defeating girl type behaviors.

BECAUSE self-defeating behaviors like fucking boys without condoms, drinking to excess, ignoring true-soul girlfriends, belittling ourselves and other girls, would not be so easy if we lived in communities where we felt loved and wanted and valued.

BECAUSE I believe with my wholeheartmindbody that girls constitute a revolutionary soul force that can, and will change the world for real."

Kathy writes,

If she were the maker instead of the muse & opened her

mouth, she would blast the notion of poetic creativity apart."

And to conclude I'd love to read you all a piece from my manuscript, "The Riot Grrrl Thing", which, in addition to writing on Riot Grrrl acknowledges Sappho and her friends as included in the Riot Grrrl fold through song/lyric lineage:

i was a libertine in

the ante-room of Love , some remember

black (earth?)
UnManageAble crux of femme

I DARED MYSELF TO MARK SOMETHING ON PAPYRI

hunk of flesh salt meat words

rush like a Maenad over

grave-isles garbage-vales thick-crocus mountains

& gut-sad seas

for Space is not easily discerned by Mortals.

hey Sapph, take up yr lyre

play something we DON'T know the words to

Gongyla,   Atthis,   Andromeda,   Amalthea

Anaktoria   &

the big violet bruise.

sing abalone-crowned Cytherea   eclipse-of-state
whose voice hustles

us   scarred   shocked   abject   subversive
UnderSung

we fight this society of death

CITATIONS

Dedication Page
rebel girl you are the queen of my world
Bikini Kill, "Rebel Girl"

Page 13
double dare ya
Bikini Kill, "Double Dare Ya"

Page 15
I think I wanna take you home
Bikini Kill, "Rebel Girl"

it's about being in love
Bikini Kill, "Outta Me"

it's all the same thing
Bikini Kill, "Liar"

Page 16
"IWentLookingForYouOuOuuu" "SoDismal"
"GoneGoneDownByTheOcean" "StartedToCry"
"GoneGone" "AnotherDimension"
"WellYouKnowWhatIMean" "IsWashedUp"
"IWentLooking"
"GirlIsWashedUp"
Patti Smith, "Redondo Beach"

Page 17
does it scare you, we don't need you
does it scare you boy
THAT WE DON'T NEED YOU!

Page 18
don't need you to tell us we're good, don't need you to say we suck,
Bikini Kill, "Don't Need You"

Page 20
I can sell my body if I wanna - god knows you already sold your mind
Bikini Kill, "Jigsaw Youth"

Is that supposed to be doing that?
Bikini Kill, "Double Dare Ya"

silence inside of me
Bikini Kill, "Resist Psychic Death"

it feels fucking blind
Bikini Kill, "Feels Blind"

Page 21
"i shall be released"
Bob Dylan "I Shall Be Released"

Page 23
"Do you really think you're ready, Buffy?"
Buffy the Vampire Slayer, Season 2, Episode 13

Suck my left one
Bikini Kill, "Suck My Left One"

Page 25
all the rage on Nothing Incorporated
Bikini Kill, "Reject All American"

Page 26
"dream-fluff donuts"
A nice little place to get donuts in Berkeley

Page 27
how punk fucking rock
Bikini Kill, "Anti-Pleasure Dissertation"

"You came back Wrong."
Buffy the Vampire Slayer, Season 6, Episode 9

"From beneath you"
Buffy the Vampire Slayer, Season 7, multiple episodes

Page 29
"girl is washed up"
"Started to cry"
"gone gone"
"everyone was singing girl is washed up"
Patti Smith's song "Redondo Beach"

Page 30
"Smiling angel."
Patti Smith's song "Redondo Beach"

Page 31
"love will tear"
Joy Division, "Love Will Tear Us Apart"

"I've lost control again"
Joy Division, "She's Lost Control"

Page 32
"outta me"
Bikini Kill, "Outta Me"

Page 35
"Spike's completely in love with you."
Buffy the Vampire Slayer, Season 5, Episode 14

"in the form of a sister"
Buffy the Vampire Slayer, Season 5, Episode 13

Page 38
it's all the same thing
Bikini Kill, "Liar"

we've got to show them we're worse than queer.
Bikini Kill, "Suck My Left One"

"My defining feeling about him was that he had never been a child but had come outta the womb a teenager. What was his zine called superstar forever."
Julie Gerstein, text message

Page 39
I EAT YOUR HATE LIKE LOVE I EAT YOUR FUCKING HATE UP LIKE LOVE
Bikini Kill, "Feel's Blind"

Page 41
I don't owe you all nothing.
Bikini Kill, "Blood One"

Who was me
Bikini Kill, "Alien-She"

feminist-dyke-whore-I'm so pretty-alien
Bikini Kill, "Alien-She"

your side of things. yeah
Bikini Kill, "Li'l Red

what are you afraid of.
Bikini Kill, "Sugar"

how does it feel, it feels blind
Bikini Kill, "Feels Blind"

Page 47
she's so very I-don't-care
Bikini Kill, "I Like Fucking"

I want it now
Bikini Kill, "I Like Fucking"

Page 49
"Happy birthday, Buffy."
Buffy the Vampire Slayer, Season 2, Episode 13

what it's like to be alive
Bikini Kill, "Demi-Rep"

Page 50
i believe in the radical possibilities of pleasure babe
Bikini Kill, "I Like Fucking"

Page 52
what the fuck is written all over your pretty face
Bikini Kill, "New Radio"

God, we're having fun
Bikini Kill, "Demi-Rep"

maybe i liked you
Bikini Kill, "Anti-Pleasure Dissertation"

I don't fit into yr dumb words
Bikini Kill, "Blood One"

Page 54
so we're going to play a new song for you & we don't know how it goes but it might work"
Bikini Kill, "Thurston Hearts The Who"

you don't make all the rules
Bikini Kill, "This Is Not A Test"

"outta me"
Bikini Kill, "Outta Me"

Page 55
"She is reputed to have been short, dark and ugly."
The Poetry of Sappho, "Sappho of Lesbos", Jim Powell, 2007.

Page 56
& I am not some lame sorority queen taking you home to meet my Daddy
Bikini Kill, "New Radio"

the you I show to you is just a lie
Bikini Kill, "Demi-Rep"

did you tell them everything I said
Bikini Kill, "Anti-Pleasure Dissertation"

"Punk must be a thing you have to get into in high school to like." Alli Warren in conversation

Page 58
"IF YOU ARE SILENT ABOUT YOUR PAIN THEY'LL KILL YOU & SAY YOU ENJOYED IT"
Zora Neale Hurston

Page 61
"a mad dash through heavenly realms" "liberated from being sourpusses" Steven Goodman in class at CIIS

Page 63
"Back it up with your life."
Lynice Pinkard

Page 64
"LOVE OVER FEAR; LOVE OVER MONEY $$$."
Lara Durback, letterpress card

Page 67
"the worst, you could say, oh, about meee ee eee, is that I'm never satisfiiii eedd ooo ooooooo oo oooo oo oo."
Janis Joplin, "Work Me, Lord"

"It's rather common, isn't it"
Amy Winehouse

"Singer Amy Winehouse died watching YouTube videos of herself after vodka binge, inquest hears."
Mail Online, 8 January 2013

Page 70
past the billboards & the magazines
Bikini Kill, "For Tammy Rae"

Page 73
What have you taught me? Nothing.
LOOK AT WHAT YOU TAUGHT ME YOUR WORLD HAS TAUGHT ME NOTHING.
Bikini Kill, "Feels Blind"

Page 74
"a steep price to pay for 20 minutes of action"
Dan A. Turner, in a letter submitted to the court before the sentencing of his son, Brock Turner. Washington Post, June 6, 2016.

White boy, don't laugh. don't cry.
Bikini Kill, "White Boy"

You really had to be there.
Bikini Kill, "Thurston Hearts The Who"

Page 77
double dare ya girl fucking friend
Bikini Kill, "Double Dare Ya"

Page 86
"Take time during the meal to enjoy the Wisdom Croissants & to talk about everyone's 'rules to live by'", Feasting with God: Adventures in Table Spirituality, Holly Whitcomb, 1996.

Page 89
"I talk too much, I laugh too loud, people stare at me when I'm in a crowd" Lois, "Strumpet"

"I WANNA KNOWWHAT LOVE IS...
I WANT YOU TO SHOW ME"
Julie Ruin, "I Wanna Know What Love Is" (which sampled "I Wanna Know What Love Is" by Foreigner)

Page 90
"You have to fight for your joy."
Nadya Tolokno from Pussy Riot, San Francisco, September 15, 2017.

Page 91
We're Bikini Kill & we want revolution grrrl-style NOW!!!
Bikini Kill, "Double Dare Ya"

Page 92
"I discovered Kathy Acker, the American writer..." Kathleen Hanna, "The Punk Singer", 2013 film.

"I hated the life which I was living at that time; I hated the society;.." Kathy Acker, Bodies of Work

Page 94
"Marginal," "experimental," & "avant-garde" are often words used to..."
Kathy Acker, Bodies of Work

"If there is a self, it's probably the world."
Kathy Acker, Bodies of Work

Page 95
"Burroughs never bores, for he & the other writers I think of as in..."
Kathy Acker, Bodies of Work

"If a work is immediate enough, alive enough, the proper response..."
Kathy Acker, Bodies of Work

I can sell my body if I wanna! God knows you already sold your mind....you think that I don't know, I'm here to tell you I do. You think that I don't know? I know the truth about you!
Bikini Kill, "Jigsaw Youth"

Page 96
I'll resist with every inch & every breath, I'll resist this psychic death.
Bikini Kill, "Resist Psychic Death"

Mama says:
You got to be polite girl You got to be polite girl
Show a little respect for your father Wait until YOUR FATHER GETS HOME.
Bikini Kill, "Suck My Left One"

"LASHES MAKE ME NO LONGER MYSELF...
LASHES, AS IF THE WORLD, BY IT'S VERY NATURE, HATES ME...
CAUSE OF LASHES: THE SURGE OF SUFFERING IN THE SOUL CORRUPTS THE SOUL..."
Kathy Acker, Blood and Guts in High School

Page 97
"The rest of THE SCORPIONS were growing the sameway I was..." Kathy Acker, Blood and Guts in High School

"I hated most that I didn't have any more dreams or visons..."
Kathy Acker, Blood and Guts in High School

Turn that song down, turn that static up, come here baby let me kiss you like a boy does!
Bikini Kill, "New Radio"

Page 98
Baby boy, you can't kill what's fucking real.
Bikini Kill, "New Radio"

I will resist with every inch & every breath
Bikini Kill, "Resist Psychic Death"

Page 98
"BECAUSE us girls crave records & books & fanzines that speak to..."
"The Riot Grrrl Manifesto" or "Riot Grrrl Is", by Kathleen Hanna, Girl Power zine, 1991. (as read by Kathleen Hanna on Vimeo, "Bikini Kill's Kathleen Hanna: The Riot Grrrl Manifesto", June 5, 2013).